Life of a Honey Badger

Sarah Machajewski

INFOMAX COMMON CORE READERS

Rosen Classroom™

New York

Published in 2014 by The Rosen Publishing Group, Inc.
29 East 21st Street, New York, NY 10010

Book Design: Jon D'Rozario

Photo Credits: Cover, p. 7 (badger) Ewan Chesser/Shutterstock.com; pp. 3, 4, 6, 8, 10, 12, 14, 16, 18, 20, 22, 23, 24 (background) Nik Merkulov/Shutterstock.com; p. 5 (badger) Rob Francis/Shutterstock.com; p. 5 (inset) USBFCO/ Shutterstock.com; p. 7 (inset) LilKar/Shutterstock.com; p. 9 Dennis Nigel/Photo Researchers/Getty Images; p. 11 Doug Cheeseman/Peter Arnold/Getty Images; p. 13 Pictries/Shutterstock.com; p. 15 (leopard) Galyna Andrushko/ Shutterstock.com; p. 15 (beekeeper) Catherine Murray/Shutterstock.com; p. 15 (lion) LeonP/Shutterstock.com; p. 17 Handout/Getty Images News/Getty Images; p. 19 (cobra) Four Oaks/Shutterstock.com; p. 19 (honey badger) Christian Heinrich/Christian Heinrich/Getty Images; p. 21 Peter Betts/ Shutterstock.com.

ISBN: 978-1-4777-2515-3
6-pack ISBN: 978-1-4777-2516-0

Manufactured in the United States of America

CPSIA Compliance Information: Batch #CS13RC: For further information contact Rosen Publishing, New York, New York a

Contents

A Fearless Animal

Have you ever met someone who seemed fearless to you? That's how other animals see the honey badger! It's known as one of the most fearless animals on Earth, and it's a strong predator, too. Very few animals are brave enough to pick a fight with a honey badger.

Honey badgers live in Africa below the Sahara, which is a very large desert. They're also found in both the Middle East and India on the Asian **continent**. Honey badgers can live in many different places, such as forests, grasslands, and mountains.

Honey badgers are mammals.
A mammal is an animal with hair and warm blood that drinks milk from its mother's body as a baby.

North America
Europe
Asia
Africa
South America
Australia
honey badger

Hunting for Honey

Honey badgers are part of the weasel family. Other animals in this family include skunks, otters, and other kinds of badgers. The honey badger got its name from the food it loves to eat—honey! It's also known as the ratel.

When honey badgers eat honey, they're actually looking for the baby bees that live in the honey and the beehive where the honey is kept. Baby bees are also called bee larvae (LAHR-vee). Honey badgers think bee larvae are tasty. Do you think bee larvae would make a tasty meal?

Honey badgers eat honey straight from the honeycomb. This is the part of the beehive where honey, larvae, and eggs are stored.

honeycomb

Honey badgers find beehives and the tasty honey inside by following a special kind of bird called a honeyguide. The honeyguide leads a honey badger to a beehive with a special call. When the honey badger hears this, it knows to follow the bird if it wants to find food. It answers the honeyguide's call with its own special growls.

Once the honey badger finds a beehive, it breaks it apart to get to the food. The honeyguide is then able to eat the honey and bugs left behind.

The honeyguide is a helpful bird.
Do you have friends who are helpful?

The Helpful Honeyguide

home	Africa and Asia
length	10 inches (25 cm)
food	honey, bee larvae and other insects, wax from the beehive
appearance	plain color, large head
skills	climbing, leading animals to beehives
relative	woodpecker
other name	guide bird

Honey badgers make the bees leave the beehive before they break it open. They do this with a very stinky smell. Honey badgers have a scent **gland** at the base of their tail that holds a stinky liquid. This liquid smells so bad it makes bees fly away from their homes!

Honey badgers are then able to break the hive open with their claws. They have very long claws on their front feet. These claws are also a **defense** to keep predators away.

A honey badger can be a very stinky animal!
What other animals are known for being stinky?

Special Skin

A honey badger looks a lot like a skunk. Its thick hair is black with a white stripe down the back. Its hair covers a short, flat body. A honey badger has four short, strong legs, too.

A honey badger's skin is loose. This helps it twist around if a predator is holding it by the back of the neck. The honey badger can then attack the predator with its strong teeth. Its skin is also very tough. It's thick enough to **protect** against bee stings and porcupine **quills**.

A honey badger's body is built to protect it from predators.

Protecting Against Predators

Honey badgers don't have many predators. Most predators don't want to get into a fight with such a fearless animal. Honey badgers have important natural defenses to scare away other animals, such as their stinky smell, tough skin, and strong teeth and claws. Honey badgers are powerful animals that other creatures usually don't like to mess with!

Some other animals still hunt honey badgers, though. Lions and leopards are common predators. Some humans also kill honey badgers to protect the beehives they use to make money.

Honey badgers aren't hunted by many animals, but they do have some predators.

leopard

lion

beekeeper

Mothers and Cubs

Baby honey badgers, called cubs, are born without the defenses adults have. When a cub is born, it has pink skin and no hair. Its eyes are also closed. It drinks milk from its mother and stays close to her until it's grown. As weeks go by, the cub begins to grow hair. When the cub is around three months old, it looks just like a smaller copy of its parents.

Cubs only live with their mother. A mother honey badger teaches her cub to find food.

Mother honey badgers usually have only one baby at a time.

Snakes for Dinner!

While baby honey badgers only drink their mother's milk, adult honey badgers eat a lot more than just honey! They eat many different kinds of animals, such as small mammals, birds, and insects. They also eat some kinds of juicy fruits. What juicy fruits do you like to eat?

Honey badgers also love to eat snakes. Their thick skin protects them from snakebites. They can even eat **venomous** snakes without getting hurt. How they're able to do this is still a mystery.

Many humans are afraid of venomous snakes, such as the Cape cobra, but honey badgers eat them without fear.

Cape cobra

Making a Home

Honey badgers use their claws to eat, and they also use their claws to dig homes for themselves. Honey badgers often live in holes, or burrows, they dig in the ground. Some burrows can be up to 9 feet (2.7 m) long and 5 feet (1.5 m) deep. Mother honey badgers dig special burrows to stay in when they have their babies.

Honey badgers also live in other places, too. They make homes among rocks, under tree roots, and in burrows made by other animals.

Honey badgers use their strong legs when they dig burrows.

Mighty Mammals

The honey badger is still a very mysterious animal to humans. Most honey badgers are nocturnal, which means they're most active at night. This makes it hard for people to watch and learn about them in the wild. Some honey badgers live in zoos, which makes it easier for people to study them.

There's still much to learn about honey badgers' powerful defenses and fearless nature. One thing we do know—they're mighty mammals that you don't want to pick a fight with! What other mighty mammals do you know?

Glossary

continent (KAHN-tuh-nuhnt) One of the seven great masses of land on Earth.

defense (dih-FEHNS) A means or method of staying safe from harm.

gland (GLAND) A part of an animal's body that makes and stores a liquid.

protect (pruh-TEHKT) To keep safe.

quill (KWIHL) A sharp, hollow part that sticks out of the skin of an animal, such as a porcupine or hedgehog.

venomous (VEH-nuh-muhs) Having or producing venom, a poison made by some animals.

Index